Teachings
of a
Not-so-perfect
mom

Glenice Lui

BALBOA
PRESS

A DIVISION OF HAY HOUSE

Balboa Press books may be ordered through
booksellers or by contacting:

Balboa Press
A Division of Hay House
1663 Liberty Drive
Bloomington, IN 47403
www.balboapress.com.au
1-(877) 407-4847

ISBN: 978-1-4525-0705-7 (sc)
ISBN: 978-1-4525-0708-8 (e)

Because of the dynamic nature of the Internet, any web
addresses or links contained in this book may have changed
since publication and may no longer be valid. The views
expressed in this work are solely those of the author and do
not necessarily reflect the views of the publisher, and the
publisher hereby disclaims any responsibility for them.

The author of this book does not dispense medical advice or
prescribe the use of any technique as a form of treatment
for physical, emotional, or medical problems without the
advice of a physician, either directly or indirectly. The intent
of the author is only to offer information of a general nature
to help you in your quest for emotional and spiritual well-
being. In the event you use any of the information in this book
for yourself, which is your constitutional right, the author and
the publisher assume no responsibility for your actions.

Any people depicted in stock imagery provided
by Thinkstock are models and such images are
being used for illustrative purposes only.
Certain stock imagery © Thinkstock.

Printed in the United States of America

Balboa Press rev. date: 09/10/2012

Wholly dedicated to my beloved family—
Jerry, Jenina, and Joshua—and to Someone
up above who loves us all. Also to all the
moms who unknowingly make the world
a better place.

Foreword

Many times, moms like me try to be everything to everyone. It makes things especially hard when we try to juggle our own personal dreams with the demands and aspirations to always be there for our families and to be able to show constant love and support. Over the years, I have learned that moms may not always have the right answers or may not always get things right, but if our actions are guided by pure and unconditional love, then nothing can ever be so wrong. Challenges are more like paths that lead to greater goodness if we'll only look at the positive side of things.

This book provides a compilation of lessons in life derived from my daily real life experiences as a mom. With this book, I hope to inspire all moms and convey the message that we have all been given an innate gift of unimaginable love that transcends any difficulties coming our way in bringing up our families. In these pages, I hope to show through my own daily life encounters that we don't have to feel bad about not being perfect because we do not have to be; we only have to perfectly love our families.

1

Monday was my son's first day at the big school. It was going so well until he realized that his mom had put white socks on him while everyone else wore navy socks. On the second day, Mom did not read the school newsletter properly—how could she miss the instructions that were in bold letters?—and she put him in the school uniform when all of the others were in their sports uniforms.

This week, I failed to teach my son how to follow school rules, but I taught him how to face adversity despite being against the flow. I said to him, "Your teacher surely remembers your name now, being the only one with white socks. If you do your best in class, she will remember you as the best boy in class with white socks."

Lesson for the day: People who succeed are not those who never made mistakes but those who learned from and made the best out of them. When you fall off a horse, the best thing to do is to get back up and ride better next time.

This week, I managed to put the wrong socks on my son, put the wrong uniform on, arrive late at school pickup, forget my daughter's school hat, go to a rugby registration when my son wanted soccer, and overcook my kids' dinner. But after a long, tiring week, my kindergarten son brought home a school merit award. So I guess someone is saying, "If you bring up your kids with pure love, no matter how you mess up sometimes, somehow you must be doing something right."

Lesson for the day: We may not always get things right, but if we wholeheartedly try to do our best, life always finds a way for us to reap the rewards.

3

Last year, I encouraged my daughter to compete in the twenty-five-metre freestyle in the school swimming carnival. Being the smallest and youngest in her level, she was very reluctant, but she went for it. She finished last. I felt so bad seeing her crushed by defeat that I cursed myself for pushing her. But I said to her, "Sweetie, competing is not always about winning but more about trying and doing your best. Surely it's better to swim with people cheering for you, even if you don't win, than just sitting on the bench. And for trying your best, to us and the people watching, you are already a winner."

Yesterday was her swimming carnival again. I felt great joy when she told me that she had not volunteered to compete in the twenty-five-metre event but that she instead competed in two events: the fifty-metre and a hundred metre. She had never swum one hundred metres before. She told me that she was not last this time, and whilst she did not win, she did her best.

Lesson for the day: The best thing we can teach our kids is to aim to do their best rather than to aim to win. This way, they end up aiming big but never end up disappointed.

One of the things I noticed about my daughter is that she is a worrier. She worries a lot about the smallest things. Last week, she kept worrying about getting into the choir after her audition. She asked me so many what-ifs and presented so many worse case scenarios that I stopped the car and said something that I had picked up from a book written by a priest named Father Orbos: "You know, worrying is like a rocking chair. It keeps you busy, but it doesn't get you anywhere." I also pulled out what I learned from the Dalai Lama: "Jenina, if your problem cannot be solved, you can worry all day and it won't change things, so why waste time worrying? And if a problem can be solved, then all the more reason not to worry. So never worry; just do your best and all will fall into place."

But speaking of being at the right place, I realised that I had stopped at the wrong side of the road so that I was blocking the other cars. One of the drivers started abusing me, but my kids and I gave the irate man a big smile and a big wave goodbye.

Lesson for the day: Do not worry. Trust that if we do our best, things may take different twists and turns, but they will eventually fall into place.

5

Yesterday, my daughter and I went to the supermarket. Whilst at the checkout counter to pay for my groceries, I noticed my car keys were gone! Thinking I had lost them, we retraced our steps. I realised in the end that the key was just in my pocket all along, but retracing my steps enabled me to remember that I also needed ginger, so it was a good run-around after all. It saved me a whole trip back to the supermarket.

Then today, I met my husband after lunch to hand over the car keys so he could go home early and pick up the kids. He surprised me with a long-stemmed rose, and I was so delighted I forgot to leave him the keys! I ended up going home early with him because I had the keys. But this turned out to be a blessing in disguise because the dozens of restaurants I tried to book were full, except one that could take us only if we started early and finished before eight. (If I hadn't gone home early, we wouldn't have made it to the restaurant in time). And as a bonus, there was a restaurant I wanted but had forgotten the name, and it turned out that the restaurant I booked was the one that I was after all along!

People might call this reckless absentmindedness.
But positively thinking, just maybe, it's nature's way
of giving me better choices than I was making on
my own.

Lesson for the day: To make the lesson simple,
believe that good things come out of misfortunes,
and if things don't go your way, maybe something
better is coming.

There is always a brighter way to look at things. Sometimes the option before you may not be perfect, but sometimes it is still worth shooting the ball because you will find that it may not be such a bad basket after all. In fact, it may be what will win your game in the end.

I have always regretted constantly missing the moms' morning teas after drop-off at my kids' school, so I vowed that this year I at least wouldn't miss the first one. Last Tuesday was the first moms' morning tea for the year. However, it was the day I had office work in the city, the day I needed to buy uniforms for my son, and the day I had deliveries for my wholesale business. I really wanted to go, so I removed all these barriers. But on the day, whilst on the way, I realised I had forgotten to bring my son's bag and my kids would be late if I turned back, so I dropped them off at my daughter's school in Cherrybrook. Then I picked up the bag in Castle Hill, headed straight to my son's school in Dural for the uniforms, dropped off the bag back at Cherrybrook, and finished off in Glenhaven for the *morning tea!*

The coffee was the best I've ever tasted, as it felt like climbing Mount Everest to get it!

Lesson for the day: All goals can be achieved with a little ounce of determination.

7

Today I walked the dog (hat 1: the dog walker); went to work (hat 2: the employee); went to church (hat 3: the Catholic); washed the dishes, helped kids with homework, and tucked them in bed (hat 4: the mom); gave the tired husband a good massage (hat 5: the wife); created a summer collection story for a new customer (hat 6: the wholesaler/artist); prepared the flyer for Life Skills Centre for Kids (hat 7 the vacation care director); emailed reminders to store sales staff (hat 8: retail store operator); wrote a note in Facebook (hat 8: the writer) . . .

I sometimes wonder how many hats one can wear in one day or how many hats fill up a wardrobe. But over the years, I've realised the wardrobe can be flexible. It expands as you put more in and more doors open; you only have to think that every glass is half-full.

Lesson for the day: Much can be achieved if we think that the glass is always half-full. Better yet, why stick to a glass when there is a whole ocean to fill?:)

Woke up late after a late night; iron broke down so my kids are wearing wrinkled shirts; husband not around to do my son's necktie, it took me fifteen minutes to work it out; nearly burned my son's lunch; didn't get to blow-dry my hair; and missed my bus. :(

My daughter said to me, "Having a bad day, Mom?" Well, I said, "No, Jenina, I am having a challenging morning. But that means I am going to have a great week ahead, because if you hit bottom early on a Monday morning, then there is no way but up!

I'm *soooo* looking forward to the sunshine. :)

Lesson for the day: There will always be a happy rainbow for someone who ignores the dark clouds and looks for the bright sunshine . . .

8

9

I was having a shower when I heard my kids rejoicing and my daughter rushed to the shower while shouting, "Thank you, Mommy. Because of you, Dad said we're going to McDo before school!" Puzzled, I said, "Why?" Then she said, "Because you burned our lunch!" That's when I realized their pie was still in the oven. I had forgotten to put the timer on!

Oh, well. At least the kids were happy, and they would definitely finish their lunch. And while this morning I failed to teach them how not to be forgetful, it is a comfort to know that I at least taught them how to always look at the brighter side of things! :)

The kids were smiling the whole way to school while holding their hash browns and sausage McMuffins for lunch. :)

Lesson for the day: There are always two sides to a situation: the happy and the unfortunate sides. The proven thing is that it is always our choice which side to chose. ☺

We often appreciate sunshine the most after a rainy day, so shouldn't we thank both the sunshine and the rain?

10

My husband Jerry and I were very sad that my son was having his first soccer practice and we could not move our meetings today. I woke up very early this morning fretting over this. I prayed so hard that my meeting would get cancelled so I could go be with my son and show support for something so dear to him.

Much to my dismay, my meeting did not get cancelled . . . But closer to the time, I got a call from Jerry with the news that his got cancelled so he could go! And that was just as well because it gave me time to stay back at work so I could work from home tomorrow because my daughter needed me to pick her up early then. :)

Lesson for the day: Someone up above has a way of saying that we should always trust that He has the best plans and knows what is best for us . . . If we do our best and pray hard, He will take care of the rest. :) Thank you, God!

An angel often drops from heaven in the least expected places when you need it the most!

11

Being a hopeless, awkward, klutzy, clumsy, forgetful girl full of bloopers, I've learned that while I cannot change how things are, I can change how I view things to stay happy. Here are my translations of some of the events in my life:

- I'm very, very busy: Don't have a dull moment.
- Have to redo my mess: Practice makes perfect.
- I cannot get it right: Life's exciting.
- My boss is horrible: My boss is teaching me how to be strong.
- I am getting old: I am getting wiser.
- I didn't get what I want: God has better plans.
- I'm very tired: I had a productive day.
- It's Monday again: Four more days, and it's Friday!
- Bad day: Wonderful tomorrow coming up, that is what sleep is for.

Lesson for the day: To be happy is a decision; we just have to look at things in a positive way until we actually believe that it is. As I read somewhere, there is always a song to those who want to sing. :)

My husband mowed the lawn, walked the dog, vacuumed and mopped the floor, cleaned the kitchen and bathroom, washed and hung clothes, played bowling with the son, helped the daughter with schoolwork—all in a days' work. Tonight he is sewing his son's uniform, as the button came off. :)

So I guess if you cannot always be a perfect housewife, you can marry a perfect houseband. :)

Lesson for the day: Moms cannot always be everything, but they don't have to. They can always move mountains with the strength and support of a loving husband . . .

12

13

I had to drive to the city today. I couldn't help but think that the whole driving experience sums up life: it may not be going as fast as you'd want, but it's moving along slowly but steadily. There are people who try to annoy you and get in your way, but if you ignore them, you'll move faster. Sometimes, you find yourself going backwards, but if you stop and rethink your course, you'll eventually work out the right way. There is no map, so it's trial and error; with a little prayer, you will eventually find the right sign. The ride is not always smooth, but at least it's exciting. And with faith, perseverance, and a sense of adventure, you'll eventually reach the place where you want to be. :)

PS, I guess it's obvious that I didn't bring my GPS. I went via the motorway, and I got lost. :)

Lesson for the day: If there is a will, there is a way.

Flexibility and adaptability are two traits I hope my kids will have. I hope that my kids will be able to talk to a prime minister intelligently and yet be able to talk sensibly and compassionately to people on the streets, that they can ride a Mercedes Benz in style but be practical enough to sit in a pedicab, be fun-loving people at the beach and serious workers at the office . . . The ability to adapt well in any environment is one of the best traits I often see in Filipinos, and I hope it will rub off on them . . .

I got to live this today. I squeezed in a quick KandyCrew customer meeting during my lunchtime, so I had to change from my corporate attire into a fashionista outfit to meet the buyer, change back to my corporate look to go back to my office, and then put on casual sneakers to pick up Joshua from his soccer practice. Now I know what Hannah Montana feels like.

Lesson for the day: If we learn to swim well with the changing flow, we will always find ourselves above the water.

15

I was awakened yesterday by the bright ray of sunshine peeping through the window. What a beautiful day! I immediately thought about a hundred things there are to do on a blue-sky day, such as a walk in the beach, a nice picnic at the park . . .

Then my husband woke up and said, "What a beautiful day for gardening." We have fifty-five trees around the house, so in my head I heard the sound *boink boink boink* like in the movies saying, 'Seriously, this is so so not the right way to spend the day'. He won, though, so we spent the morning pruning trees followed by doing a hundred other house chores . . . I surprisingly ended the day feeling happy and contented.

Lesson for the day: A beautiful day is not a condition; it is a state of mind. It is not about what you do but what you accomplish. It is not about where you are but who you are with. So it's definitely a beautiful day today and every day!

Happiness is not a condition; it is a state of mind.

16

As soon as I heard my son had broken his arm, I rushed to see him and vowed to be his source of strength. But as soon as I saw his condition, I burst into tears (another *boink boink boink* event as this was clearly not the plan). My son must have sensed my breakdown as even whilst in pain, he kissed me as if to say, "I'm OK now that you are here, Mom, but are you?"

From then on, I was amazed that he would bubble about how lucky he was to have a moving trolley bed, how fun it was to be riding in a wheelchair, and how cool his plaster was, like Ironman.

So I guess I didn't turn out to be his source of strength. He turned out to be mine.

Lesson for the day: Parents like us will never be able to shield our kids from all pain and hardships, but if we are able to bring them up to be positive and resilient enough to withstand all storms, then we have planted sunshine throughout their lives.

My daughter said to me the other night, "Mom, when I grow up, I would like to work for your accounting firm, then put up my own business and save money so I can sleep all day." It baffled me why she would want to sleep all day, but she probably meant she was aiming to retire early. So not a bad goal to start with.

I know, though, that what she wants will still change many times over, so when she turned to me and asked, "What would you like me to be?" I wanted to say, "I want you to be a lawyer, a diplomat, a philanthropist, etc." But I bit my lip because what I said might change her life forever. So I said, "My child, I would like you to be whoever you choose to be. All I will pray for is that you try to be the best in whatever you do."

Whew! I hope it was the right answer. And that "the prize is right."

Lesson for the day: As parents, we should not predict or dictate what our kids will turn out to be. All we can do is to help bring out the best in them.

17

The best way
to succeed is to
be happy with
what you have
and to turn it
into something
better.

I said to my husband, "Jerry, I would like us to stay home for a quiet day." That day, I woke up early to walk our dog, Bobo; had an hour walk with my daughter Jenina; did the groceries; made a big breakfast of bacon, mushroom, roasted tomato, and toasted bread, then cooked five dishes for our week's food; baked banana bread; helped Jenina make bibingka (a Filipino-style bread) for a school project; cleaned the kitchen; helped the kids with homework; gave the kids a bath; prepared dinner; ironed clothes for the week; tucked the kids for bed; and now I'm ready to relax and watch a movie while folding clothes. What a "quiet" day!

Lesson for the day: I learned somewhere that if people feel dog tired, it is only when they growled all day . . . I laugh off any chore, as I learned to never count how much work you need to do but to always count the blessings that come with it . . . :)

18

19

Planned to attend a Superclassmum Networking session for women in business at 7:30 today, so I woke up really early, prepared the kids for school faster than a speeding bullet, and then, when I reached the venue, the door was closed. I called the organizer who answered like she just had gotten off the bed. I found out the time was p.m. and not a.m. Clearly, I don't belong to the Superclassmum when I can't even read the invite properly. I went straight back home, but since I brought the new car, I don't have the house keys so I can't go in the house either. Oh, well. I have back-to-back meetings today, so maybe Someone is saying, "It's a beautiful day I have for you today, take some quiet time to bask in the beauty around you."

Lesson for the day: At times, we have to relax and enjoy the beauty around us, because then we will see things more clearly. :)

Today is ladies' day out. To be able to make it, I woke up at 5:30 to walk the dog, ironed the kids' uniforms, prepared breakfast, folded and put away laundry, bathed the kids, and cooked lunch in record time—what a mom will do for a massage, spa pedicure, and high tea!

It's really been a great day with the company of wonderful mums. Thank you, ladies! Special thank you to my husband who had to look after six kids so I could go out . . . That was better than any valentine gift. :)

Lesson for the day: Some goals may be difficult to achieve, but if we work really hard, it makes the taste of success even sweeter.

20

21

Things I learned from my five-year-old:

1) Ask the question five times and you will get the answer you need. Six Sigma promotes the same principle. It took them years to come up with this idea, they should probably have just asked kindy students. :)

2) Always make a counter-offer, this is the best way to test your opponent's (and in this case your mom's) boundaries.

3) Always take the riskiest option (like picking a knife over a toy). That is the fastest way to know what won't work.

If I had learned from him when I was in university, I would have become a great lawyer.

Lesson for the day: It might sometimes be maddening to work out how a child's mind works, but sometimes, if we look at the positive side, we might actually learn from them valuable lessons in life too.

You know you are overworked and need to slow down when . . .

- Someone has to talk to you twice before you hear what he or she is saying.

- You fall asleep in front of someone you are talking to. (Yes, it happens!)

- You can never finish watching a movie on TV because the only time you don't dose off is when there is a laptop on your lap.

- Your only quiet time for planning life is whilst driving, such that you forget you still have passengers to drop off.

- Your main means of catching up with friends is through Facebook!

I cried a lot yesterday because my daughter's classmate's father died, and I didn't even know him. It made me remember life is short. We must make sure every moment with the people we love is what we want them to remember us by . . .

Lesson for the day: Never forget to live, laugh, and love. :)

22

23

I came across a book recently that says there are foods that naturally make people feel happy because they contain tryptophan that converts to serotonin, which brings out that feel-good feeling. Examples of the happy foods are bananas, tofu, spinach, beans, and pineapples.

This morning, I feel happy. Is it because everything fell into place? I had my three-kilometre run, a shot of wheatgrass, a glass of freshly squeezed orange juice, and completed packing parcels for my wholesale customers. The kids are well, and I am still on track to make my 8:30 am meeting in the city.

Or maybe it is the banana I had this morning . . . Well, whatever it is, I still plan to eat more bananas when I get to work and hand out some to grumpy people I might come across! :)

Lesson for the day: We don't have to find happiness; it is in the simple, everyday things around us.

For as long
as we
appreciate
the little
blessings that
we have, we
will always be
given more.

24

We've started putting up the Christmas decors and I was going to finish it today, but there was one box of decors I could not find. I looked everywhere. I ended up clearing up a lot of the cabinets, sorting the kids' toys to give to charity, and organising our office in the hope that the box would turn up. I was exhausted by the end of it and was about to give up, till I finally found the box. It was inside the Xmas tree box, *he he he* . . .

Oh, well. Someone is probably saying that I should really do the house pruning, as I had been putting it off forever and it took a missing box to make it happen.

Lesson for the day: Believe that things happen for a good reason. Sometimes, when things are not going our way, it is probably leading us to achieve more than what we originally hoped for.

I have finally been able to watch the movie *How Does She Do It?* and, just as I expected, most of us working moms can relate to it. I felt like I was seeing myself in motion in the movie, except that I don't look like Sarah Jessica Parker and I don't have a boss that looks like Pierce Brosnan. (How I wish!) There is the military operation in the morning whereby you have to be out the door by a certain time or all of your schedule will be out of whack, there is also you and your husband constantly putting up a business case as to who has the more important meeting, and the feeling of being so out of place with moms who you see at school in Mer-C and joggers ready to go to the gym after dropping off to the teacher a beautiful, home-made cake or home-sewn quilt. And worse, the broken promises to your children . . .

I think what is hardest for moms who live a double life is attempting to make like normal for the family—wanting to still do things yourself rather than getting a nanny to do your job, being at all your kids events no matter what, cooking real food rather than frozen ones, bringing to school a self-crafted hat for the school parade and a home-baked cake rather than ready-made ones from the supermarket . . .

25

And I guess, as Sarah Jessica has learned by the end of the movie, mom's got to do what she's got to do that will give her self-fulfilment. It could be staying at the house 100 percent or going for the career that she's after. Fulfilling your own dreams is as important as helping everyone else in the family fulfil his or hers. The boundary though to me is that no success will be worth anything without my family. So it might be hard, but I will chase my dreams but never give up my family time . . .

Success today: doing a photo shoot for KandyCrew and the kids' homework the night before, I was tempted to give the kids ready-made nuggets for their lunch and ready-made cupcakes to take to the school's cupcake day, but no . . . I made them a burrito with veggies and made my first decorated cupcake ever. It can be done. :)

Lesson for the day: Moms should not feel guilty chasing their own dreams. We all have competing dreams to strive for. Moms just have to know what's most important to live for . . .

Jenina said to me this morning, "Can Aunty take us to school, because when you do, we are always late?" Feeling indignant, I said, "Well, today I won't hurry you up. You take your pace and you will get to school as quickly as you prepare yourself. I won't make you wait till I finish getting ready. As soon as you are ready, we go. Your destiny is in your hands." I ended up having to drive them without brushing my hair and changing clothes so I could live up to my promise.

Everything was a rush to get them out the door. The only time to relax was in the car that I started daydreaming until I heard Jenina say, "Mommy, you missed the turn. Now we will be late." Oh, no, the saga continues. So I said to Jenina, "Ooops, sorry. But don't worry. There is another way." So I made a turn in what I thought was another shortcut, then I realised another, "Ooops. It's not the way I had in mind" I proceeded pretending I knew where I was going while in my head I was panicking 'coz I only had ten more minutes or Jenina would be late! Then I heard Jenina say, "Oh, wow, Mom. This way is much quicker. We should really take this route every day. "I was thinking, *Really? I still don't know where we are.*" Then I saw a familiar corner and worked out the way . . . :)

26

I then said to Jenina in a very confident (albeit slightly pretend) tone, "See, Jenina . . . Sometimes, we may get things wrong. When it happens, no use stressing. The better way is to work out how you can make things right, and you never know. It might lead you to an even better way you never even knew existed. :) *Whewwwwww!*

By the way, we made it to school in time. :)

Lesson for the day: We can be bitter or better; the decision is always ours . . . We may not always get things right, but we can always turn things into something good . . .

Would you prefer to be a better wife or a better mother?

Charlene Gonzalez is a former Philippine beauty queen and the wife of my teenage favourite celebrity, Aga Muhlach—I know that gives away how old I am. Her answer goes like this: "Whilst it is hard to answer, I would say I would prefer to be a better wife. This way, my husband will be happy, which will make us both happy, so as a result we can be better parents. Then I will be a better mother anyway.

I thought that it was a really good answer, such that it made me think, *"OK, Charlene, you do deserve to snatch Aga from us,* Not that we stood a chance, *he he he."* It would have been a perfect answer to a Q&A in the Ms Universe Pageant. Before hearing this though, I would have given a different answer (which explains why I'm not a beauty queen . . . LOL!)

But thinking more about the question, I am now inclined to agree with Charlene. Many times, I have heard marriages break because the mother focussed so much on the child that she neglected the husband, but I have never heard an instance where the mother loved the husband so much that she neglected the fruit of their love: the children.

27

Ergo, to love the children does not necessarily mean loving the husband/wife, but love for husband/wife automatically converts to loving the children. So I concede, another new mantra: love thy husband first and foremost. :)

Lesson for the day: As the saying goes, the best gift a parent can give to children is to love their mother/father.

While my kids are very young, I will teach them first about dreaming big. Life is full of possibilities to those who strive hard and do their best. :) However, later in life, the mantra I will teach my children: live for today, plan for tomorrow, yes, but never at the expense of enjoying the present.

I'm exercising my new mantra this morning. I plan to run tomorrow, but this won't stop me from enjoying my big breakfast today. :)

Lesson for the day: Dream big and work hard for tomorrow, but never forget to live for today.

28

29

My New Year's resolutions this year . . .

1) I will prepare a to-do list each day and I will only use one notebook for them. I already prepare to-do lists, but I have about a dozen notebooks that I use so I never really know which one is current.

2) I will actually use my to-do list. Often I will prepare a list of groceries but not bring the list with me to the supermarket.

3) I will put my keys and wallet in the same place in my bag so it's easy to find them. I've always designated a place for these but never actually put them in there.

4) I will categorise my work papers and have a folder for each of them. I've always had the folders but never really actually segregated the papers.

5) I will finish what I started before I move to the next. I often start ten things at the same time and end up ten things being late.

6) I will stay away from sweets (every now and then, maybe).

7) I will eat everything but in moderation. I will eat more fruits and veggies each day and do more exercise. I can almost hear my daughter say, "Now, Mom, really?"

8) I will pray and help the community more.

9) I will only buy because I need the item and not because the item is on sale. :)

10) I will be good to my husband. (Joke?) :)

This is a long-term programme, though so like any project, expect delays. I'm not perfect, will never be, but will forever at least try. :)

Lesson for the day: We may not be perfect, but the amount of success we achieve often comes from the decision to try . . .

To be a good example to children, moms should first be continually inspired and then move to being inspirational.

I read yesterday an article about one of the richest women in the world. It was an article about the endless legal battle between her and her children over money. Not forgetting that she also had that battle against her own dad and stepmom, I must say it was incredibly disturbing to hear about a family that has enough money to last them for more than a few lifetimes, yet they are still fighting and unhappy.

Then I learned that her kids grew up in a very expensive boarding school overseas, and apparently it is typical of billionaires to send off their kids to boarding schools from their young age. This is a great puzzle to me. I work hard so I can give my kids a good life and have time to spend time with them, so if I have all the money in the world to give them a good life, why would I send them to boarding school where they would be away from me most of the time?

While I'm all for giving children the best education, should parents ever let education get in the way of them being able to spend time with their kids? I don't think they should. I send my kids to the best school I can afford, but I also believe that the guidance that parents can give to their children can never be equalled by the most expensive schools in the world. And more than anything, kids need to feel the love of their parents, especially during their vulnerable years, so their constant presence is what's important.

30

If being rich means missing out on the daily dinner chats, the banters while dressing kids up each day for school, the bedtime stories, or the weekend playtime with the kids, then it is a curse to be rich after all.

To me, what makes people the happiest is the priceless bonding time with their families. So thanks to the article about this filthy-rich woman, more than ever, I resolve never to let ambitions get in the way of being with my family. I resolve to dedicate my time to raising my kids so they grow with the love and support of family around them all the time. I believe that it is all that they need and all that I need to be happy. I won't ever aim to be rich; I will only aim to have a happy family. And for all of us moms and dads who have worked this out, I think we are richer than this woman because we have everything right here, right now, that all her money cannot buy.

Lesson for the day: If we want our kids to grow loving and caring, we have to show them love and care. What they need are not material things but our constant presence and show of love. The worst thing is to be very poor in spirit because all we have is our money.

Two years ago, I felt so bad when I sweet-talked Jenina into competing in swimming and she finished last. Last year, I felt good because she decided to join on her own, and while she did not win, she did better. The truth is I never thought that she stood a chance because she is the smallest and the youngest in the class and does not get to swim much. This year, she joined the competition again, and this time she won silver. What makes me happiest is that today my daughter learned two of the best lessons in life: the first step to success is *trying* and what gets you there is *perseverance*. Things get so tough that even I start to doubt this sometimes. But my daughter taught me and reminded me that this is still so true. I only have to remember today.

Lesson of the day:The first step to success is **trying**, and what gets you there is **perseverance.**

45

I often run five kilometres with my husband, and because I am not a gym junkie like him, he always has to sweet-talk me to keep me going. He often says, 'Do not chase five kilometres. Chase one at a time and then don't stop. Before you know it, you have made it to five.' And it works. What I learned from that is that small goals make big things happen if you keep going.

About the Author

Glenice Lui is a woman of many hats. She owns a children's wear label, KandyCrew, which supplies to approximately one hundred stores across Australia; runs a retail store at the Rouse Hill Town Centre in Sydney; operates a vacation care centre called Life Skills Centre for Kids; and works part time as a senior manager in the IT advisory division of one of "the Big Five" accounting firms. She is a member of the church choir and the church's rosary group. More importantly, she is the mom of Jenina, ten, and Joshua, eleven, as well as the loving wife of Jerry Lui.

Printed in the United States
By Bookmasters